Photographing America

Photographing America

Know the Land and the People[©]...through Photography

Edited by George Hornby and the Editors of

EASTMAN KODAK COMPANY

CROWN PUBLISHERS, INC. · NEW YORK

Copyright © 1976 by Eastman Kodak Company
and Crown Publishers, Inc.

ISBN: 0-517-52585-8
Published simultaneously in Canada by General
Publishing Company Limited
Designed by George Hornby
Printed in the United States of America

Library of Congress Cataloging in Publication Data

Main entry under title:

Photographing America.

    Includes index.
    1. Photography. 2. United States—Description and travel—
Views. I. Hornby, George. II. Eastman Kodak Company.

TR146.P443   770   76-13553
ISBN 0-517-52585-8

Title Page photograph by David Muench

FOR ALL WHO TAKE PICTURES
BOTH AMATEUR AND PROFESSIONAL:
THEIR CAMERAS ARE THE
EYES OF MEMORY

Phil Marco

Table of Contents

Introduction

YOU ARE OPENING the pages of a book which we hope you will find to be truly an album of the American land and American life . . . *your* land and *your* life. In the first section we have tried to capture in photographs the day-to-day life of people like ourselves and you and your family—at home, at worship, at school, at work, and at play. While doing this, we have woven into our text and captions pointers on how you can best preserve in pictures your own precious records of infancy, childhood, growing up, maturing, and reaching the serenity of the older ages.

Throughout the book, you will find specific capsules of photographic data that, taken together with the pictures themselves, give a short course in personal photography. Remember that many of the pictures here are the work of serious amateur photographers. Not only are these good technically, but they have special qualities of spontaneity, humor, and storytelling. Many others are by the finest of professionals—these give you pictures to treasure and targets to shoot for. And also remember that one of the best ways to learn to *make* good pictures is to *look* at good pictures.

Some of the best pictures in this book were chosen from entries in the yearly contest held by Kodak in cooperation with local newspapers in the United States, Canada, and Mexico. Because of our theme, we limited ourselves to entries from this country, but we still could have filled several books with warm, touching, amusing, and amazingly well done photographs. For the 1975 Kodak International Newspaper Snapshot Awards approximately 300,000 snapshots were submitted to 98 newspapers for local judging. Of these, 698 were selected for final judging which resulted in 247 winning shares of the KINSA '75 prize jackpot of $55,000. Certainly this evidences the deep and widespread interest in personal photography.

Later in this book we take you on a tour of the towns and villages of America and of her great cities, large and small. What we show here can be your guide to the photogenic high spots of places near you and places you may sometime visit. Too, all the photographic know-how demonstrated in this section can help you in photographing your own and other areas by showing you what to look for and how best to photograph it when you find it.

This segment includes the vacationlands—those man-made or man-developed attractions meant for family fun and relaxation and the placid hideaways for camping and fishing or just lazing. For that special vacation that every family should have a chance to take, we include a broad range of views of the magnificent natural wonders of our national parks and monuments. The unbelievable majesty of these settings will be infinitely more meaningful to you and your family when you put yourselves in the picture. The inclusion of a child or two in a scene in Yosemite National Park or at the Grand Canyon not only does not take away from the subject but, rather, puts it in scale and furnishes counterpoint to the awe that it inspires.

In the last section of this book we visit the past of America and, in a very real sense, its future. For, when you see and photograph the places where our history was written and the memorials to the men and women and events of our two hundred years of growing, you will sense your own place in this history and you will find feelings of durability, of security, and of hope for the future of America.

A Note on Cameras, Film, and Technique

Have you ever wondered why some photographs are more appealing than others—why some turn out to be great favorites while others eventually are filed away and forgotten? In this book we're going to show you hundreds of outstanding pictures and talk about what makes many of them good. We'll also discuss those pictures that you'll be taking and how you can improve them by understanding a little about composition, lighting, and camera handling.

The medium of photography continues to provide photo enthusiasts with cameras that are more automatic and more fun to operate. Nowadays it's possible to capture your good times in snapshots, color slides, and even sound movies simply by picking up a hand camera, aiming, and pressing the shutter button. You don't really need complicated photographic equipment. Good pictures can be taken with any camera in most daylight situations. For snapshots and slides made indoors or at night outdoors, you can use flash and stay within the recommended flash-to-subject range (usually between 4 and 9 feet away). In the realm of home movies, high-speed color film and fast camera lenses have nearly eliminated the need for bright and often unpopular movie lights, while automatic exposure control has taken the guesswork out of obtaining well-exposed images.

Others who favor the versatility of adjustable cameras with features such as interchangeable lenses, a wide range of shutter speeds, and built-in rangefinders, can explore more imaginative, interpretive approaches to their photo hobby. The picture possibilities available open new horizons in picture-taking.

Whether you carry a camera in your pocket, around your neck, or mounted on a tripod, your goal is really the same—to capture some aspect of life around you on film so that it can be viewed and enjoyed again and again in the future. Cameras and film, then, serve as the means to this end result. The quality of your pictures depends, in part, on how well you understand and take advantage of your equipment.

Involvement is another key factor in your quest for better pictures. After learning all the possibilities and limitations of your camera, accessories, and film, take the time to observe carefully the scene you're photographing and select the best camera angles. Study the lighting. Notice the color of the light, observe the angle at which it falls on the subject, and study the depth and form of the shadows it casts. Be willing to experiment—to try, try again.

You'll discover that your awareness of good composition and lighting, along with your knowledge of proper camera handling, will increase rapidly as you gain experience with your camera. This experience will teach you a great deal about how to make better pictures, and soon the mechanics of picture and camera control will become as natural to you as adjusting your television set.

Enjoy the many fine pictures in this book and remember the photo tips it contains. Then take your own camera off the shelf, reacquaint yourself with its potentials, and get going on making your own personalized photographic story of America!

Neil Montanus

PART ONE

America / The People

Sonja Bullaty

Family Portrait

Throughout American history the family has
been an all-pervasive thread, tying
together and giving continuity to our ways
of life. Not dynasties, not the capitalized
Family, but the family next door. The
family just like us that can be so
different from us in all but the basic
realities. So long as the family survives, so
will the community and the country.
Looked at this way, the simplest of family
albums is a true archive, preserving as it
does your own image in the great picture
of the growth and perpetuation of a nation.

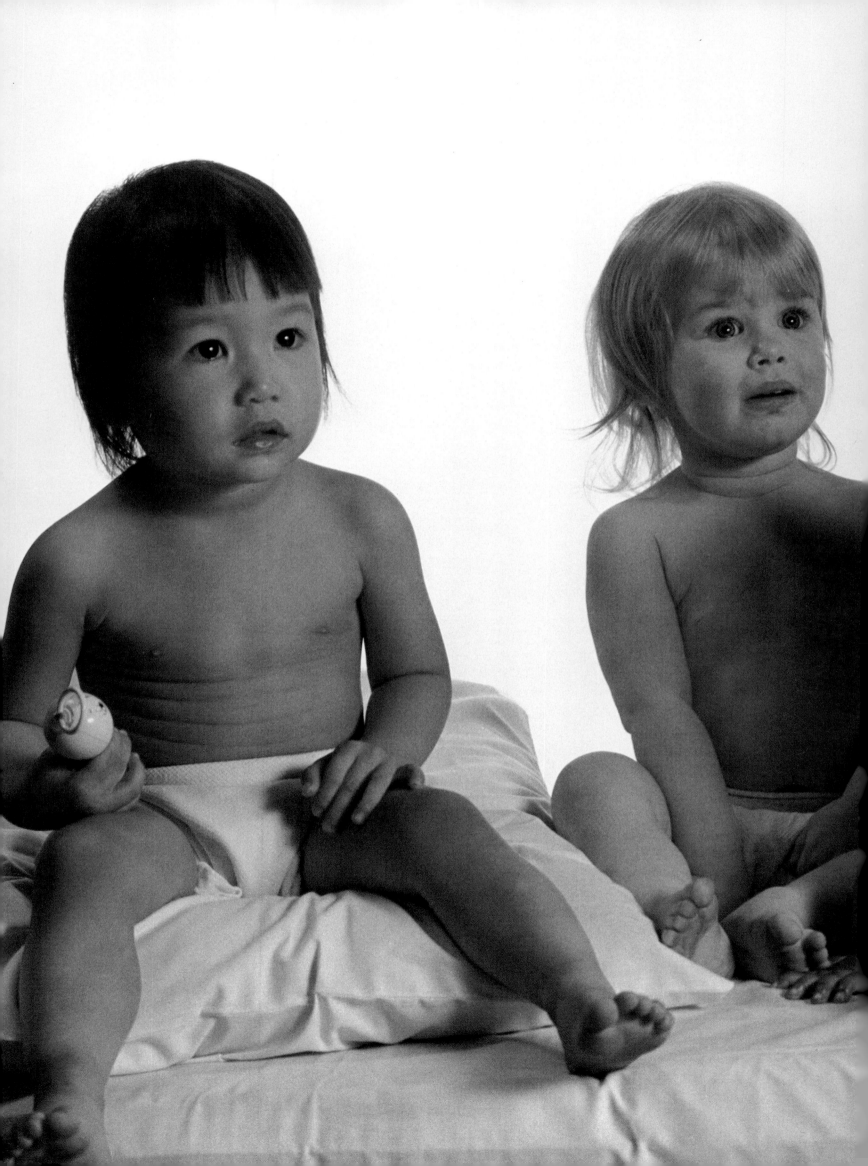

Rev. Patrick Hannon

Perhaps one of the reasons why so many artists and sculptors *and* photographers have chosen to portray this subject is that its warm touch of human interest lends itself so well to any creative medium. When you try picturing it yourself, try for a picture that will live up to the innate beauty and joy of your models.

Mother and Child

Pictures of babies are easy and fun to take because babies are so expressive. A simple prop such as a ball or stuffed toy can evoke enough cute expressions to fill a baby book or Grandma's album with pictures. Keep your camera loaded with film and in a convenient place around the home so you'll be ready to catch the baby's impromptu activities.

James Kendall, M.D.

Don Maggio

Be Familiar With Your Equipment. Use a camera-and-film combination that you've used before. If your camera requires batteries for flash pictures, make sure that the batteries are fresh. You might want to carry an extra set of fresh batteries along, just in case. Start out with your camera loaded and have your extra film and bulbs readily accessible. You don't want to miss an important moment because you're busy looking for supplies.

Watch the Light. Daylight coming in from a window can produce a natural-looking informal portrait of the baby. But if the lighting in the room is too dim for your camera to handle, be prepared to use flash.

H. Halma

Princess Royal

Move in Close. Close-ups of babies (or any subjects) are nearly always more interesting than distant shots. Try to fill your viewfinder with your center of interest.

Keep the Background Simple. Try to choose a camera viewpoint that provides a plain, uncluttered background. "Busy" backgrounds, with lots of distracting detail, make your picture look disorganized and can draw attention away from your center of interest.

She will grow up in a democracy, but let us not begrudge her a few months of the regal life. Spoiled by her loyal subjects and snug on her pillowed throne, she literally cries out for the services of the royal photographer.

Mrs. Robert Dale Hoepner

Keep 'Em in Place. Occasionally, you'll need plenty of patience to get good pictures of children because they seldom stay in one place for very long. Ask another family member to play with the child while you take pictures. You'll get the added bonus of a good picture of both of them as they enjoy each other's companionship.

Bob Clemens

Share Your Pictures. Your family and friends are all interested in seeing pictures of your children so share your best pictures with them. Have extra prints and enlargements made of your favorite snapshots. You can order additional prints for relatives and friends. Take your negative, slide, or photo into your photo dealer and outline your needs. The dealer will take care of the rest.

Emiel Blaakman

Carol J. Maihori

Keep Your Eyes Open and Your Camera Loaded

Don't miss all of the moments of truth that crop up, usually at inopportune times. You can't film them all but you can try. If you come to think of your camera as an extension of your eyes, you will catch many a memorable scene that no amount of planning or staging could create. The laugh, the smile, the tear that these snapshots evoke will pay you well for your alertness.

Thelma S. Myerson

Gary L. Wincott

Dean Stroud

Stirrings of Art in America

Doris Barker

Phoebe Dunn

It's not important that any of these budding geniuses grow up to be a Grandma Moses or a Norman Rockwell. It *is* important that you capture on film their willing or unwilling early efforts.

Emiel Blaakman

Josef A. Schneider

Victor Szovati

Gladdies Meyerhoff

Jerome Flinkman

Emiel Blaakman

Josef Schneider

Barbara Jean

Get Down to the Baby's Level. The best level for baby pictures is the baby's level. From this viewpoint, you can show the baby's face, which is much more interesting than the top of his or her head.

Bruce Smith

Double Exposures

CHILDREN AT PLAY—in any location, at any time of day, in any weather—can provide you and your camera with a world of enjoyable picture-taking possibilities. Snap them while they're relating to each other and busy having fun.

Hold Your Camera Steady. Camera movement spoils more pictures than anything else, so get a good grip on your camera and gently squeeze the shutter release.

Moving Subjects. If your subjects are swinging, seesawing, walking, or otherwise moving around while you're trying to get the picture, try one of the following techniques for sharper pictures:

1. Choose a viewpoint where the action will be coming directly toward you or going away from you.
2. Snap the picture during the split second of suspended action. For example, if a child is on a moving swing, there is a moment just before the swing starts to change direction during which there is little motion.
3. The farther a subject is from the camera, the less apparent any movement will be. Avoid tight close-ups if you can't use one of the action-stopping techniques mentioned above.

Two can be a crowd if the two are a pair of photogenic children. One piece of advice. Get your pictures before they realize that they're co-starring in a major film production and start hamming it up.

Ronald Bloomquist

Bernard Faingold

David La Claire

Al Gilbert

Champ Hosley

Though Young: Studies in Dignity

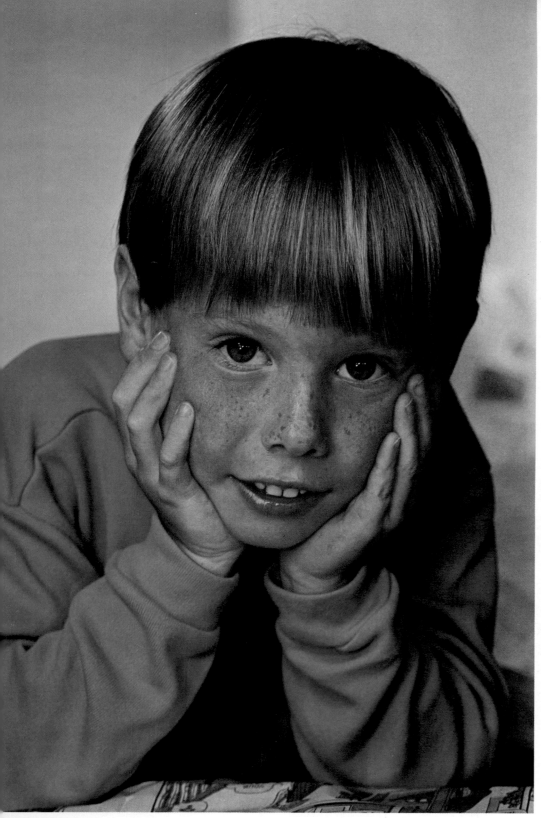

John Mechling

28

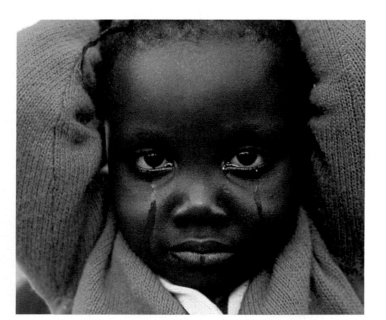

Jerry Johnson

Suzanne Szasz

A Child Is Many People

And all of those many people have many
different moods. The more moods of this very
complicated member of your family that you
can capture, the more you will remember and
understand him or her later on.

29

SOME OF THE MOST treasured pictures of children show them doing the everyday things of life. The baby modeling her brand-new bonnet or secure in the arms of her mother, Junior attempting to ride his first two-wheel bicycle, Sis trying on mom's old clothes—all these things make good picture subjects. Keep your camera handy and take pictures of the everyday events that make up the times of your life. Then, to make your images stand out photographically, practice these picture-taking tips:

Fill the Viewfinder. Moving in close to your family members is an excellent way to make your pictures better. Close-up pictures of children (as well as adults) are more interesting because you can see their expressions. With most nonadjustable cameras, you can get as close as 4 feet (1.2 meters) to fill the camera viewfinder with your subject. With a focusing camera, you can often get as close as 2 feet (.6 meters). Check in your camera manual to see how close you can get.

Think Color! Color can add plenty of interest to your snapshots of children. When taking their pictures, you can control the color by selecting clothes for them to wear. Choose warm and vibrant colors to make your subjects stand out against foliage or a blue sky.

Jon Abbot

Glenn Fishback

30

Neil Montanus

M. Peterson

Life Looking Out from a Face

And what a face! Every hope of the world
shines from her eyes. Looking at her, you feel
that for today, at least, to be alive and to be
beautiful is enough.

William A. Himmelstein

What It's All About

Jon Abbot

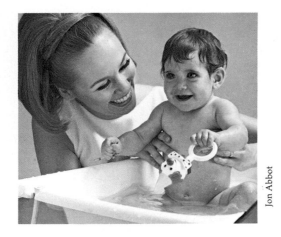

Tell a Story With Your Pictures. The next time your little one decides to paper the wall with strawberry jam or spread lipstick from ear to ear, take not just one but several pictures of the memorable occasion. Almost all childhood activities—a trip to the barbershop, birthdays, Christmas morning under the tree, or even the bath—lend themselves to telling some kind of story. To get complete coverage and make your editing job more fun, follow these tips:

- Start taking pictures early, before things get going.
- Get pictures of everyone involved in the activity, either by themselves or in a group.
- Snap some close-up pictures of the action in full swing.
- To wrap up the story, take a finale picture. This could be a shot of the child asleep on a mountain of thoroughly enjoyed toys, a food-covered face, or the entire gang gathered around the birthday table.

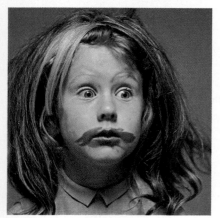

Emiel Blaakman

Neil Montanus

Baby Pictures Never Grow Old

Witness these two examples. Except in the
matter of wardrobe, you would have no way of
knowing that the picture above was taken
almost forty years ago. It's still a great picture
and certainly might win a prize today as it did
then. The picture opposite won first prize for
black-and-white in the 1975 KINSA
competition.

Bennet Greenberg

Dennis Hallinan

"Barefoot boy with cheek..."

Mrs. G. Downing

Blessings on thee, little man,
Barefoot boy with cheek of tan!
With thy turned-up pantaloons,
And thy merry whistled tunes;
With thy red lips, redder still
Kissed by strawberries on the hill;
With the sunshine on thy face,
Through thy torn brim's jaunty grace;
From my heart I give thee joy,—
I was once a barefoot boy!

JOHN GREENLEAF WHITTIER

38

David LaClaire

Doris Barker

Susan M. Netz

What Generation Gap?

Is Everybody Happy?

Emily Wheeler

William J. Mareth, Jr.

Carole Bright Stober

Nonchalance

You've Heard of the One-room Schoolhouse

But chances are you've never seen one. There are not many left like this one-room schoolhouse in Stehekin, Washington. Located in the heart of the Lake Chelan National Recreational Area, the village is inaccessible except by plane or boat, and its residents are Park and Forest Service employees, guides, a writer or two, and one schoolteacher. The teacher has eleven students, one of them his daughter. He teaches eight grades of elementary school in his one-room log schoolhouse.

The Gift Horse

Photographs by Gary Welpley

Mark Daughhetee

Sheer Exuberance

James R. Howard

Studies in Silhouette

Gilbert B. Witten

Gary Welpley

46

Lee Howick   Neil Montanus   Joe Reynolds

Gary Welpley   Emiel Blaakman   Gary Welpley

Music Comes to America

Milking Time

The Old
Swimming Hole

Bobby Adams

Norm Kerr

Norm Kerr

Philip James

She Walks in Beauty

Wayne Barber

Pete Culross

Tony Petrocelli

Peter Gales

Dining Out in America

Whether it's a backyard cookout, a picnic in a
nearby park, or a real back-to-nature campfire
meal, here is your chance to see yourself as
host, chef, and gourmet. Put one of your guests
to work with a camera and later you can relive
the occasion . . . and add weight to nothing but
your ego.

53

One Nation Under God

Most religious occasions and ceremonies
should be inviolate, but there are times when a
quick, unobtrusive snapshot can record the
moment for your album. Try to catch the
feeling, the great or simple grandeur of the
scene. No camera can really do more than
capture the image. The spirit has to come from
the viewer when he or she looks at the great
altar of New York's St. Patrick's Cathedral or
the simple Mormon family in Star Valley,
Wyoming, saying grace over a meal, most of
which was raised or grown on their little farm.

Gary Welpley

Type of Color Film. The illumination in houses of worship may be primarily tungsten or daylight, depending on how much light the windows let in and the time of day. Choose the appropriate type of color film (daylight film or tungsten film) for the predominant lighting.

Al Gilbert

WEDDINGS are among those special occasions in your life that are certainly worthy of pictures, plenty of pictures. Since you'll naturally want the best and most complete pictorial coverage possible, contact a professional wedding photographer. He or she is trained to capture the highlights of the occasion and can produce excellent, professional results. You should depend on the professional for the formal wedding pictures, but you may want to supplement this coverage with an informal picture story of the occasion.

Plan Ahead. Make a list of the pictures you especially want to snap. Talk to the bride for ideas. She'll know the photos that the professional photographer will be covering, and you can arrange to take the pictures that are not on the schedule.

Check With the Minister. It isn't appropriate to take pictures during a church service. However, you may be able to take a candid picture as the bride comes down the aisle as well as some posed photos after the ceremony.

Select Your Camera Location. Pick positions in the church and reception hall that will allow you to be unobtrusive and yet aid you in capturing the best pictures. Get as close as possible to your subjects and use the least distracting background available.

56

Monte Zucker

Here Comes the Bride

Leon Kuzmanoff

Cameras Never Forget Anniversaries

Stock up on film in advance, tie a string around your finger and, when the day comes, snap plenty of pictures. Every anniversary deserves an album or slide sequence all its own. And why not a wall or alcove decorated with enlarged prints? What better way of counting your blessings.

PICTURES OF FAMILY GROUPS probably rank highest among your cherished photo keepsakes. These are the pictures you'll treasure for years—in your family album, enlarged in a frame, or carried in your wallet. To get the best possible pictures when photographing your clan the next time they gather together, here are some simple tips:

Bring Them Together. For an informal group portrait with plenty of interest, arrange your subjects close together. A close grouping lets you move in close with your camera, showing bigger faces in the resulting picture. Moving in close also reduces any problem of a distracting background and centers the attention on your subjects.

Subject Placement for Flash Pictures. When using flash, try to keep the distances between the subjects at a minimum so that all the subjects will receive about the same amount of light from the flash. When people are far apart (near and far), chances are those close to the camera will look too light in the picture and those far away will look too dark. Only those people in the middle will appear just right.

Peter Gales

The Glorious Fourth

J. Waring Stinchcomb

Fireworks

FIREWORKS DISPLAYS are easy and fun to photograph. You'll get the best pictures of aerial displays if you put your adjustable camera on a tripod and capture several bursts in the same picture by making a time exposure. Focus your camera on infinity and aim it in the direction of the display. Exposure is not critical. A larger lens opening will make the lines in the burst thicker and lighter; a smaller lens opening will make the lines thinner and darker.

　　If you don't have a tripod for making time exposures, you can get successful results by hand-holding your camera and using an exposure of 1/30 second at $f/2$ on a medium-speed film such as KODACHROME 64 Film. Take your pictures when the fireworks bursts are at their fullest.

C. Joffe

Theodore Ehernberger

Carl Dumbauld

Allan De Loach

David Lichtenstein, Jr.

Robert Chaet

Ted Ase Daniel

Hallowe'en!
Night of the Jack-o-lantern

62

Neil Montanus

The Most American of Holidays

Thanksgiving is the family holiday when the generations get together and the wanderers return. Dissension and diet are both forgotten on this day just as they were in the times when the Pilgrims and the Indians sat down to peace and plenty and forgot for a time their everyday hardships.

Bill King

Dick Boden

Christmas Is a Time of Memories

Tony Petrocelli

If you have never photographed your family's Christmas, make sure that someone in your house gets or gives a camera this year . . . with plenty of film and flash. Christmas evokes memories that should be treasured on film. It is perhaps the most exciting picture-taking holiday of all. It has everything: color, suspense, sentiment, love, surprises—and a captive cast of characters.

Lee Howick

Emiel Blaakman

Keith Boas

R. J. Boden

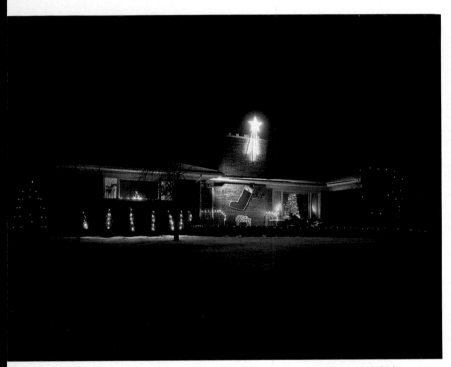

Neil Montanus

Neil Montanus

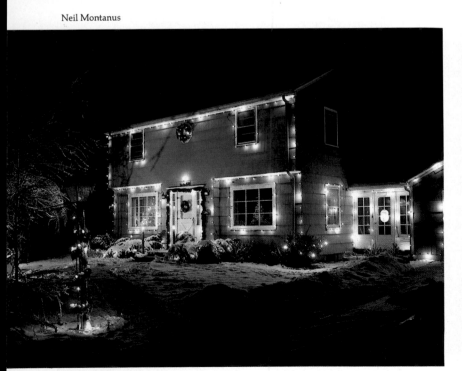

Photographic Greeting Cards

You PROBABLY HAVE people on your greeting card lists who are seen less frequently than you'd like. A photographic card, by including a special personal touch, adds an extra measure of warmth to the seasonal wishes you extend to these people. These cards are especially valued when there are children in your family. A picture, as nothing else, keeps your friends closely in touch with the growing-up process.

Take Your Pictures Early. Maybe you already have a picture that is just right for a photo-greeting card. But if you haven't one, now is the time to get out your camera. When you're planning a Christmas photo-greeting card, pictures showing people dressed in winter clothing and enjoying winter activities can be just as seasonal with or without snow. Props such as a carefully placed bough of greens decorated with an ornament or two, some candles, a wreath, or a few pinecones will provide the needed seasonal touch. On the other hand, the pictures you use for Christmas photo-greeting cards don't really need a christmas or winter theme. A picture of your family with a background of fall foliage can make a colorful card.

Take Good Pictures. The photograph is the heart of any photo greeting, so the better the picture, the better the greeting. The most personal and most appreciated picture you can include in a photo greeting is a picture of you and your family. To help make your pictures of people interesting and effective...

- Keep your subjects busy
- Add color
- Move in close
- Choose the best viewpoint
- Keep the background simple

Ordering Cards. Once you've taken the picture, all that's needed for a good photo-greeting card is a good negative, slide, or print. Your photo dealer will help you select a greeting-card design and will take care of the details for you—even to supplying the envelopes.

James Sadler

George Butt

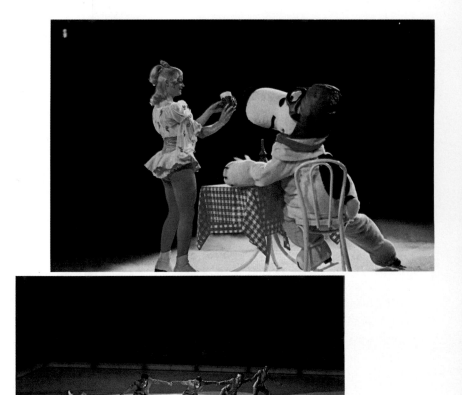

Fun on Ice

CIRCUSES AND ICE SHOWS are well lighted and can usually be photographed by existing light if you have an adjustable camera with a fast lens and high-speed film. Lighting is provided by two general kinds of light: carbon-arc spotlights and general tungsten lighting. Daylight film gives the best color rendition for acts lighted by carbon-arc spotlights, while tungsten film usually gives the most natural color rendition for scenes illuminated by the overall lighting of the arena. When colored filters are used over the lights, both types of film will give equally good results.

Photographs taken at the Ice Follies
by Emiel Blaakman

Photographed at the Ice Capades by Keith Boas

Photographs taken at the Damascus Shrine Circus
by Jim Dennis

The Big Top

Your Garden
Can be a Joy Forever

A BLOSSOM may live for only a few days in a garden, but it can live season after season in a picture. Pictures preserve the intricate detail and delicate beauty of flowers, so you can enjoy them over and over again.

Take Close-up Pictures. The most fascinating pictures of flowers are close-ups, and you can take close-up pictures with your still or movie camera. You can get as close as 4 or 5 feet (1.2 or 1.5 meters) from a flower with almost any camera. You can take extreme close-up pictures with the help of an inexpensive gadget called a close-up lens. Close-up lenses fit over most camera lenses like a filter, and they allow you to take pictures closer to the subject than the normal focusing distance. Your photo dealer can help you select the close-up lens you need to fit your camera.

H. Mayer

John Hood

The Background. Learn to study the background. It's easy to overlook, but it will be in your picture. Use viewpoints that give you a plain or uncluttered background. For example, for low-growing flowers, try aiming the camera almost straight down and the ground will be your background. If you want a dark background that lets the flower stand out in contrast, ask a friend to stand so that his or her shadow will fall on the background (but not on the blossom). The background will look dark in the picture. To put a sky background behind a tall flower, hold the camera low and aim it upward.

Lighting for Flower Pictures. Check to make sure the flowers are not in patches of shadow. If possible, change your position to find flowers that are completely in the sun or in the shade.

In sunlight, take pictures from an angle that allows the sun to shine on the side or back of a flower. The highlights and shadows created by sidelighting help emphasize the shape of a flower, and backlighting reveals the translucent beauty of the petals.

On overcast days or in the shade, the lighting is soft and even. As there are practically no highlights and shadows, you can record all the detail in the center of a bloom. Use a high picture-taking angle on overcast days to keep the dull sky out of the picture.

Keep your flash unit handy when you go out to take flower pictures. When there isn't enough light to take a picture in daylight or indoors in conservatories and at flower shows, use flash. Be sure to stay within the flash distance range given on your camera or in your camera manual.

Barbara Jean

Pete Culross

Norm Kerr

Stephen Douthat

Helen Kittinger

James Boorn, Jr.

Lee Howick

Norm Kerr

Walter Chandoha

Walter Chandoha

Treat Your Pets Like "Family"... Take Their Picture

Harold Ferguson

PETS are among the most appealing subjects for pictures. Photos of soft, furry kittens, a youngster romping with the family dog, or the cat curled up in a sunny window will have a fond place in your family album.

The Pet's viewpoint. You will get the best pictures of your pets by getting down to their level. Pictures taken from the pets' viewpoint will show their faces, which are much more interesting than the tops of their heads.

Don Baxter

Fill the Viewfinder. Sound familiar? Well, we just can't say this often enough. Your close-ups of any subject will be more interesting than most distance pictures. Try to fill your viewfinder with the important subjects. For very small pets like birds, hamsters, and kittens, you may want to use a close-up attachment. Check your camera manual to see if close-ups are possible with your particular equipment.

Use a Plain Background. Cluttered backgrounds will detract from the pet, while plain backgrounds will show off the subject better. Outdoors, use a low camera angle for a blue-sky background. Or try a higher angle to use green grass or foliage as your background. Indoors, arrange your pet in front of a plain wall.

Keeping Pets in Place. Try enlisting the aid of a friend or a member of the family to play with the pet while you take pictures. You'll get the added bonus of a good picture of both the animal and the person having fun with each other. If the pet won't cooperate, have your helper hold him and take a picture of both subjects.

Wayne Thompson, Jr.

Michael Herrel

Bob Clemens

Pete Culross

Walter Chandoha

76

Bob Clemens

Neil Montanus

Norm Kerr

Peter Gales

Doris Barber

Chris Schuler

William Cottman

Neil Montanus

Mrs. Richard Stanton

78

Jim Pond

For Want of a Horse

Howard Foote

Photographing Fish

PICTURES OF FISH make colorful and unusual additions to your collection of pictures. Fish are small so you'll need a close-up lens for moving in extra close to the tank.

The lights on most fish tanks aren't bright enough for picture-taking purposes, so use flash. When you use flash at close distances, cover the flash reflector with a handkerchief to cut down the light. Shoot at a 45° angle to the front of the tank to avoid reflections from the glass.

Pete Culross

Pete Culross

Tigers In the House...

Eugene Wagner

Peter Gales

Neil Montanus

Pete Culross

Peter Gales

Frank Cowan

Howell Conant

Peter Gales

Emiel Blaakman

Jon Abbot

Great Moments in Sport

Oops!

Michael Charles

Marvalee D. Feikert

Once in a Lifetime

Pete Culross

Frozen Action

A good hockey game, or even a bad one, can give you some beautiful snapshots. If, that is, the organized mayhem on the ice doesn't keep you from organizing yourself.

William Hill

Stopping Action

THE BEST WAY to "stop" action is to use a high shutter speed. Exactly how high depends on how far you are from the action and in what direction the movement is traveling with reference to your camera. Remember that things moving at right angles to the camera require higher shutter speeds than those moving toward or away from you or diagonally. You can stop distant action, such as a football play in mid-field, with a slower shutter speed than you'd need for the same action occurring only a few yards away. Every sport has "peak" spots where action is temporarily halted or slowed.

A shutter speed as slow as 1/30 second will "stop" people walking slowly toward the camera, while a fast sprinter running diagonally past the camera would require at least 1/500 second. Generally speaking, use the highest shutter speed that the lighting conditions will allow.

Sometimes, breaking the rules produces more convincing results in photographing action. Action pictures taken at high shutter speeds freeze the movement so effectively that occasionally the photos can look static and lifeless. To overcome this effect, you can use the panning technique to give the impression of great speed. Swing your camera smoothly and keep the subject centered in the viewfinder as you make the exposure. The finished picture will show the moving subject "stopped," but the background will be a racy blur. The slower your shutter speed, the greater the background blur. It's a good trick to remember for dark days when you need to expose color film at slow shutter speeds.

Paul Johnson

Lee Howick

Point of View

Peter J. Colosi

Leo M. Johnson

Game Called

Tennis, Everyone?

John Bickel

Or a
Session of Squash

Anthony Giraulo

Good Clean Sport

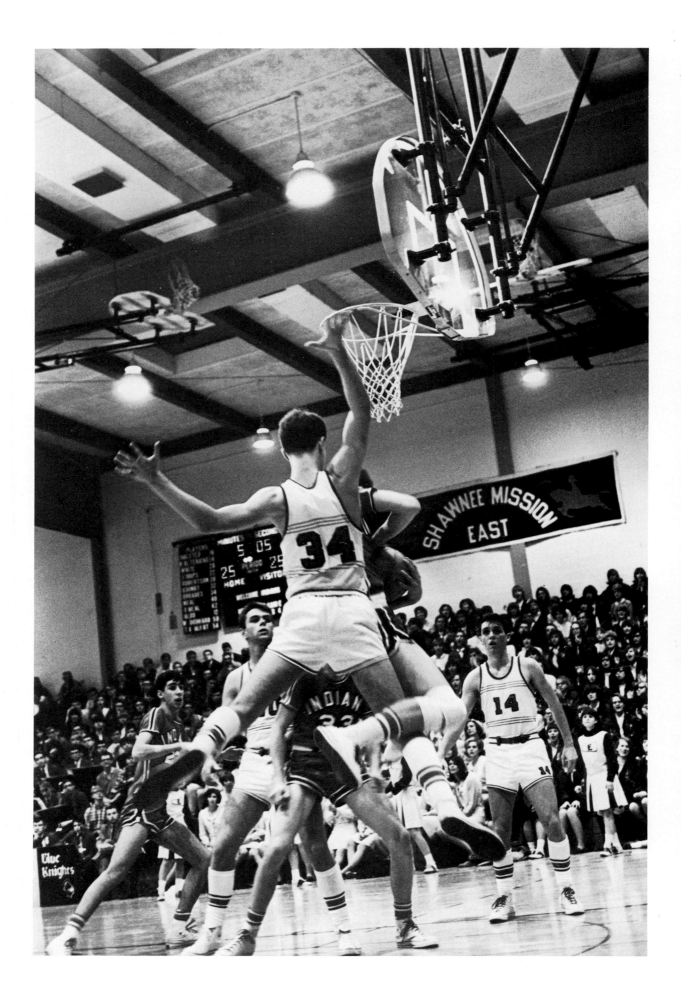

Photographs by Gary Welpley

Old Baseball Players Never Strike Out

Certainly not if they play for the Three-Quarter Century Softball Club of St. Petersburg, Florida, better known as the world-renowned "Kids and Kubs." These two teams play three or four games a week, and their season runs from Thanksgiving time until springtime, when most of the players go back north to visit their grandchildren, great-grandchildren, or, in a few cases, their great-great-grandchildren. You see, to qualify for a spot on one of these teams you must be at least seventy-five years young.

America on Two Wheels

Peter Gales

Caught in the Act

H. G. Trainer, Jr.

A Study in Dejection...

but Wait Till Next Saturday

A Neglected Heritage

98

Myron Sutton

Perhaps we grew too fast as a nation to protect
and preserve the culture and color of the
Indians who were here before us. It may be too
late, but some Americans are now trying to
remedy this. Giving your children even a
surface glimpse of Indian life may spark their
interest and encourage them to delve deeper
into a sad but fascinating part of our history.

George L. White

Best of Show

Jane Stephenson

The Horse Next Door

102

Faces on the Land

It's become a cliché to say that one picture is worth a thousand words. These few pages of character studies without a word of text should prove that there is nothing wrong with a good cliché. And nothing really wrong with America.

Jack Newsom

David Richard Stockton

Mark Alan Bretheim

Gene Claseman

Jim Dennis

Jim Dennis

Gary Welpley

Walter Chapelle

Dan Tucker Kamin

Jay Stock

Norm Kerr

Song of the Open Road

Afoot and light-hearted I take to the open road,
Healthy, free, the world before me,
The long brown path before me leading wherever I choose.

   * * *

I think heroic deeds were all conceiv'd in the
   open air, and all free poems also,
I think I could stop here myself and do miracles,
I think whatever I shall meet on the road I shall like,
   and whoever beholds me shall like me,
I think whoever I see must be happy.

         WALT WHITMAN

Photograph Overleaf by Lou Parker

PART TWO

America / The Land

H. Wendler

The Peaceable Kingdom

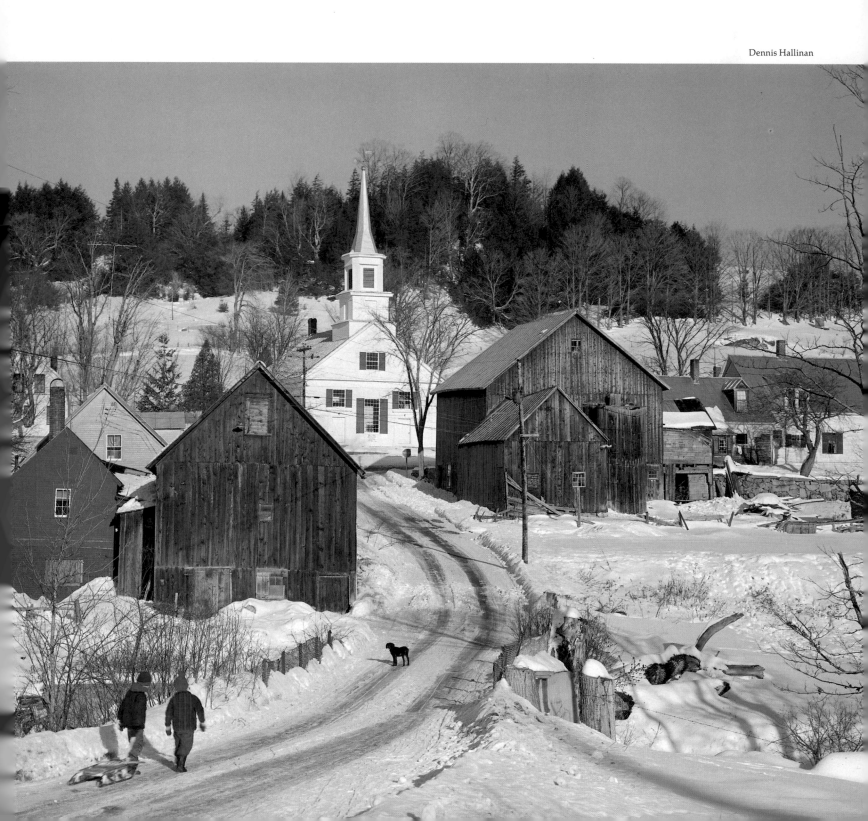

Esther Henderson

Lee Howick and Neil Montanus

Dennis Hallinan

When Nature's Palette Overflows

Overleaf

Portland Head Lighthouse was the first lighthouse authorized in the United States and is the oldest lighthouse in America in continuous use. It was erected in 1791 on orders from George Washington.

Photograph Overleaf by John Fish

A Day in the Life of a Lobsterman

Nemo Warr

Life on the Bounding Main

Phoebe Dunn

A Picture Can Be a Poem...or a Symphony

F. Wendler

Dennis Hallinan

The House by the Side of the Road

Albert A. Kunigisky

The Beauty of Clean Line

Philip Krug

Shelden Berdé

Barbara Jean

Glen Saw Lwin

James Howard

Eric G. Stewart

Accidental Masterpieces

Alan J. Burt

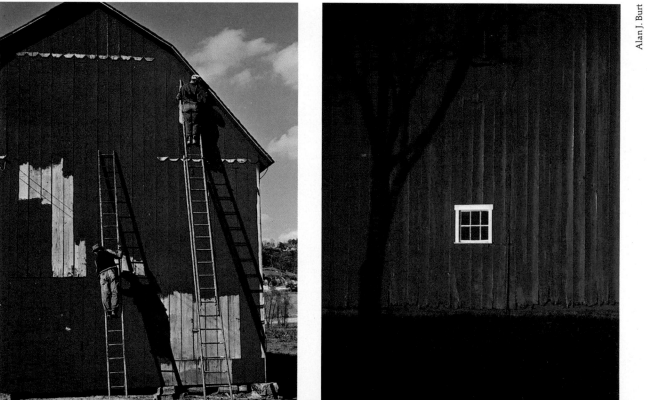

131

Glenda Jackson

Inside Looking Out and Outside Looking In

Arthur D'Arazien

America has always been a nation on the move and in a hurry. We invented the mass-produced automobile, then built 3.7 million miles of roads to drive on. We invented the airplane and set up more than 280,000 miles of airline routes. But the story of our country's expansion begins with the railroads. The first railway in the U.S. was the Baltimore & Ohio, established in 1831. It was followed by giants such as the New York Central and Pennsylvania. More than 30,000 miles of track were laid before the Civil War.

The Singing Rails

Hank Mayer

Rodney Stevens

There's a Big World Out There

Dennis Hallinan

Sunsets

Dennis Hallinan

BRILLIANTLY COLORED pictures or slides of sunrises and sunsets are breathtakingly beautiful. Fortunately, they are among the easiest pictures to take, because exposure is not so critical. Overexposure makes the sunset appear lighter and earlier, while underexposure gives deeper, richer colors, making the sunset look more advanced. A typical exposure for a setting sun partially obscured by clouds would be 1/60 second at ƒ/5.6 for KODACHROME 25 Film (Daylight), or 1/125 at ƒ/5.6 for KODACHROME 64 Film (Daylight) or KODAK EKTACHROME-X Film.

When you use an exposure meter, the reading should be based on the brightness of the sky and clouds. This will render the foreground dark and the sun slightly overexposed, with rich colors in the clouds. Any objects such as trees, buildings, or people appearing in the foreground will be silhouetted against the sky to form a dramatic frame for the subject.

George Herczegh

Gaylord Morrison

Norman W. Schumn

Out of the Mist

Underwater Photography

MORE AND MORE people are imitating fish in these days of snorkels, swim fins, and scuba tanks—and they're taking their cameras with them. To take pictures underwater, you need some specialized equipment and a new set of picture-taking rules.

Waterproof Housings. The prime requirement is some sort of waterproof housing for the camera which will keep it safe and dry and at the same time allow easy operation of its controls. Underwater housings can be anything from a simple rubber or plastic bag with a transparent faceplate to a complex cast-metal housing costing as much as the camera it contains. Some cameras are specially designed for underwater photography and don't require an underwater housing.

Color Compensation. Underwater, the red in the spectrum is quickly absorbed by the water, so underwater pictures will appear quite bluish. At a depth of less than 30 feet (9.1 meters), you can use a filter such as a KODAK Color Compensating filter CC30R to reduce the strong blue cast. When using the CC30R filter, increase exposure by 2/3 stop.

Refraction. Another change that takes place is that your camera lens no longer "sees" the same field of view as it does in air. The refraction of light rays through water magnifies everything slightly, so that objects appear to be only three-fourths of their actual distance away. Consequently, you have to get farther away from your subject to get it all in the picture. Since the refractive index of water affects your eyes in the same way that it affects the camera lens, you can judge distance underwater just as you do above the water so you can disregard the magnification effect when focusing the camera.

Exposure. Underwater exposure depends on the type of day, angle of the sun, depth of the subject, turbulence of the water, and color of the bottom. That's why a camera with automatic exposure control works so well for underwater photography.

Photographs by Neil Montanus

James L. Ames

You Could Hear an Anchor Drop

144

Bernard Faingold

Day's End

Birds—
Shyest of Models

THERE ARE men and women who have devoted their lives to the patient art of bird photography. You may not want to go so far as to build yourself a blind or a tree-nest, or invest in telephoto lenses and other sophisticated equipment. Too, you may not be willing to rise before the birds. But you can still get a great deal of pleasure and satisfaction from "capturing" on film the occasional feathered show-off who alights at your feeder, the strutting robin stalking worms on your lawn, or the photogenic gull perched on a pier or hovering over the water.

Paul D. Yarrows

Allen Vella

Dr. J. Spies

146

Donald Cornelius

Robert Leppard

147

Ralph Amdursky

New York: The Melting Pot

At the United Nations

Photograph Overleaf by Ralph Amdursky

Ralph Amdursky

Times Square, U.S.A.

O. J. Roth

Neil Montanus

Fifth Avenue
on St. Patrick's Day

Albert Kleiman

Cityscapes

Tony Petrucelli

William Hudson

154

Daniel D. Leahy

Jeannine M. Matthews

Mrs. Howard Marlin

Hurry, Hurry, Hurry!

Neil Montanus

Pictures of Scenery

NATURE'S wonders are among the most popular of all picture subjects. Fortunately, they're also among the easiest things to photograph well. Oftentimes the difference between ordinary results and good results may be very small. Niagara Falls will never be mistaken for a drippy little 5-foot cataract in any picture, but merely having someone in the foreground will help communicate its size.

Experienced photographers even carry extra bright-colored clothing along, just to be sure that the people in their pictures will be colorful.

The Falls of Niagara

157

Ralph Amdursky

On the Beach at Fort Lauderdale, Florida

Exploring the Everglades in Style

Ralph Amdursky

John Zimmerman

The Way of a Man with a Boat

160

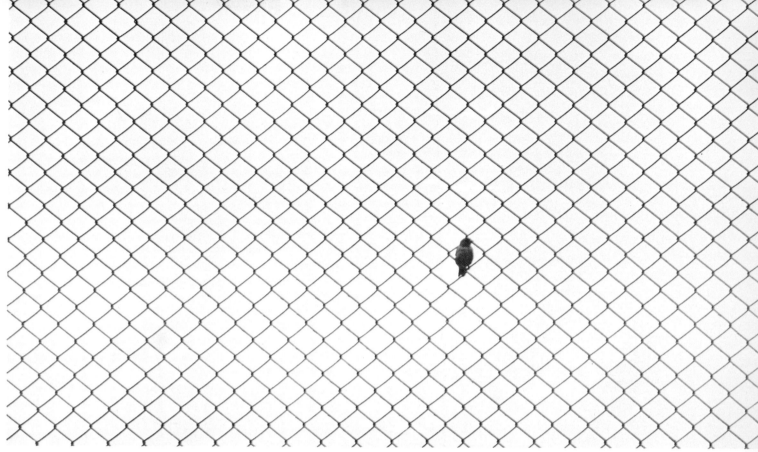

Martin Rogers

Sitting Pretty

Jeffrey S. Stephan

Cypress Gardens:

Photographer's Eden

John Fish

H. R. Thornton

Reverence

164

Rev. T. Piotrowski

Reserve

Reverie

Arthur K. Dugan, S.J.

Charles M. Mason

Gilles Chamberland

Be It Ever So Humble

"Jazz will endure as long as people hear it through their feet instead of their brains."

—JOHN PHILIP SOUSA

The most American and enduring music is jazz. Not swing, not the cool jazz of the fifties and sixties, but the hot jazz of King Oliver, Jelly Roll Morton, and Louis Armstrong. New Orleans jazz, or Dixieland, grew out of black folk music, spirituals, and blues combined with turn-of-the-century marching music. It quickly spread from the French Quarter to Chicago, New York, San Francisco, and other distant cities, ushering in the Jazz Age. Almost any night a band of venerable musicians delights foot-stomping enthusiasts by playing traditional Dixieland jazz at Preservation Hall on St. Peter Street, near legendary Basin and Canal Streets.

Neil Montanus

New Orleans: Home of Dixieland

Keith Allen Jones

The Watchers

Robert Piehl

Harold Mann

Esther Henderson

Herb Jones

Pause for Reflection

Tom Algire

CREATING UNUSUAL PICTURES is a never-ending challenge and one way to enter the world of creative photography is to capture abstractions on film. There are any number of techniques to produce photographic abstractions in color—some complex, others amazingly simple.

One easy technique for creative interpretation involves reflections. Take pictures of the world around you as it reflects in commonplace things like the nearby pond, a mirror, the curved bell of a band instrument, or the chromed surface of an automobile hubcap. These pictures require no elaborate photographic equipment, no special lenses, filters, or trick attachments—only the selective, imaginative eye of the person behind the camera.

Start carrying your camera more often, keeping a lookout for unusual shapes, patterns, and, of course, reflections. You'll soon have a whole collection of thought-provoking images worthy of display and favorable comment.

Bob Clemens

Barbara Jean

Emiel Blaakman

171

Carl Blesch

The Worker and the Playboy

W. C. Donoho

Bob Clemens

George Eastman House, Rochester, New York   Emiel Blaakman

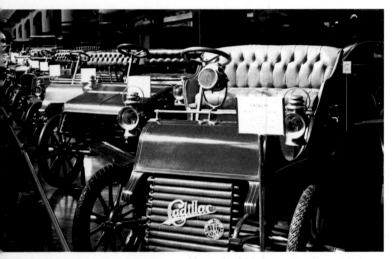

Henry Ford Museum, Dearborn, Michigan

The Museum of Modern Art, New York

The Cloisters, New York

Bob Clemens

174

Bob Clemens

Buffalo Bill Historical
Center, Cody, Wyoming

Rod Grimes

Neil Montanus

Rod Grimes

Air Force Museum, Dayton, Ohio

Museum Pieces

George R. Wooliver

Random Shots

176

James B. Keating

Little Boy Lost

Heigh Ho! Come to the Fair

There's something for everyone at the county fair. Tap your savings, wear comfortable shoes, pack your family and your camera in the car, and off to the fair. If there's not room for family *and* camera, you'll have to decide which to take.

O. J. Roth

O. J. Roth

Walter Chapelle

Tom McCarthy

Walter Chapelle

179

Ray Atkeson

Winter Wonderland

Ozzie Sweet

Overleaf
Jackson Hole, Wyoming
Photograph by Neil Montanus

San Francisco: City by the Bay

Creating a Mood

Barbara Jean

Bill Harley

The Complete Angler

Ralph Amdursky

Waikiki Beach: Season in the Sun

Mickey McGuire

Shades of Tom Sawyer

"We said there warn't no home like a raft, after all. Other places do seem so cramped up and smothery, but a raft don't. You feel free and easy and comfortable on a raft."

MARK TWAIN

Keep Shooting in Any Weather. Anyone could (and should) shoot this marine scene on a clear day. But, when the fog rolls in—if you have a camera with an f/5.6 or wider lens opening—you can still take pictures and capture a moody scene like the one on the right. Bad-weather pictures offer a change of pace.

Place Your Center of Interest Off Center. Pictures look less static and more pleasing when the subject is slightly off center. Mentally divide the scene into thirds, both vertically and horizontally. Place your center of interest at one of the four places where the lines intersect. Of course, "rules" like these are made to be broken—some subjects look good when they're centered in the picture area. But most often, an off-center composition looks best.

Keep the Horizon Straight. If the horizon is at an angle, your subject will appear to be sliding off the picture. Avoid dividing your picture exactly in half, with the horizon right in the middle of the picture.

Wilderness Heritage

When people think of America, they often picture sprawling cities, skyscrapers, crowded highways, factories, in short, all the trappings of an advanced civilization. But there is another America . . . an America of lakes and streams, mountains and valleys, wildflowers and wild animals. And thanks to many Americans who cared, we in the age of computers and rockets, can retreat from the noise and smog of the city to the quiet, refreshing beauty of the country . . . to an American wilderness.

Photograph Overleaf by Esther Henderson

PART THREE

America / The Wilderness Preserved

Ansel Adams

A Matter of Balance

The Forest Primeval

There are higher mountains, larger lakes, longer rivers, and denser forests elsewhere in the world. What makes the face of America unique is not superlatives but its spectacular variety.

Peter Gales

Kay Lombard

When Nature Lets Off Steam

Joseph Atchison

The Sensuous, Subtle Sands

David Muench

Giants Come in All Sizes

Bunchberry

Virginia Bluebells

Bunchberry

Amanita

Partners in survival are the massive redwood and the minute wildflower. And the flower may well say to the tree what the elf said to the boy who laughed at his small size: "I'm quite as big for me as you are big for you."

Photographs by John Fish

Large-flowered Trillium

Strawberry Bush

Jewel Weed

Hepatica

Witch-hazel

Sundrops

Bellwort

Jack-in-the-Pulpit

Wake Robin

Monkshood

Dutchman's Breeches

California Poppy

"Trees" of the Desert

Josef Muench

Josef Muench

Norm Kerr

Norm Kerr

George Ingram

Tally O. Bowman

Tally O. Bowman

Nature as Sculptor

Carl E. Moser

Edge of the Wilderness

Moods and Majesty

Overleaf
The Grand Canyon
Photograph by Fred Ragsdale

Hank Mayer

Peter Gales

L. H. Benschneider

Get People in the Picture

Yosemite National Park

Dennis Hallinan

L. H. Benschneider

Devil's Tower

Peter Gales

Grand Teton National Park

213

214

Making Titles
as You Travel

EVERY HOLLYWOOD EPIC has titles—and so
should your picture stories. Titles help you
organize your pictures and make them
more interesting. Titles also help explain
your photo record and add a change of pace
to your presentation. It's easy to make titles
on picture-taking excursions or at home.

Titles can be the simplest things
imaginable, such as roadside signs, historical markers, or even advertising billboards.
Almost any state or national park has a sign
naming the park and others marking the
various attractions within the park. As you
travel around, take a picture of each of
these signs. It will help keep your audience
with you on your travels and remind you of
which pictures were taken where.

A little ingenuity will produce any
number of clever and functional titles. For
spur-of-the-moment titles, try writing in
the sand or spelling out words with sticks
and stones on the ground.

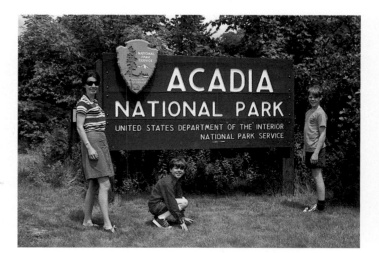

Yellowstone National Park

Depth of Field

DEPTH OF FIELD is the distance range between the nearest and farthest points in a picture which are in acceptably sharp focus. By manipulating lens openings or focus settings and subject distances, you can increase or decrease depth of field. The focus setting on your camera, as well as the lens opening, controls depth of field. The closer the subject is to your camera and the closer the focus setting, the less depth of field you have at a particular lens opening. And the smaller the lens opening (the larger the *f*-number), the greater the depth of field at a certain distance.

Many adjustable cameras have built-in depth-of-field scales on their lens mounts. These handy scales indicate the near and far limits of sharp focus at any combination of lens opening and focus setting. Creative use of your depth-of-field scale will enhance your pictures. By controlling depth of field, you can emphasize or play down any part of the picture. For example, you can place great emphasis on foreground objects by having the background out of focus.

Chiming Bells   Lichen

Move in as close as your camera will focus.

To help your main subject stand out have someone create a background shadow with a jacket or blanket.

Place the horizon high to suggest closeness, low to suggest spaciousness

Sometimes you can capture a shadow and use it to direct attention toward your center of interest.

217

Calypso Cascades, Rocky Mountain National Park

The Falls of Yosemite

White Mountains National Forest, New Hampshire

218

Longs Peak
Rocky Mountain
National Park

M. Roberts

Alaska: The Mendenhall Glacier

A Rain Forest in the State of Washington

Ahrens

The Oregon Shoreline

Ray Atkeson

Lonesome Buffalo

Myron Sutton

Jack Zehrt

Overleaf
Robertson's Windmill, Colonial Williamsburg
Photograph by Keith Boas

PART FOUR

America / The Past Revisited

A full-scale reconstruction of Fort James. The original was built in 1607.

The tower of Jamestown's Church, built around 1639 once served also for protection against Indian attack.

The Jamestown Settlement

Jamestown, Virginia—the first permanent English colony in the New World. In reconstructions and in actual remains you can get an idea of Jamestown as it was when the original settlers, some dating back to 1607, made this spot their home.

Photographs by Keith Boas

Colonial Williamsburg

From 1699 to 1790 Williamsburg was the capital of Virginia and a cultural, social and political center ranking with Boston, Philadelphia and New York. Restored to its eighteenth-century appearance this mile-long historic area has within it more than 500 buildings and nearly 100 lovely gardens.

An 18th Century Garden

The Wigmaker's Shop

The Palace Gardens

The Governor's Palace

Exterior photographs by Keith Boas

231

Chowning's Tavern

Ezra Stoller

The strikingly modern City Hall with Faneuil Hall in background

Boston and
its Environs

Replica of the *Mayflower*

Bunker Hill monument

Replica of the *Beaver*, a Boston Tea Party ship

Minuteman statue in Lexington

Paul Revere statue

Paul Revere's grave

The Old State House

Replica of Concord Bridge

233

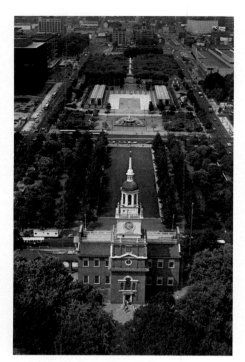

View of Independence Hall

Washington's Headquarters at Valley Forge

Valley Forge Memorial Arch and re-created soldier's hut

Benjamin Franklin National
Memorial in the rotunda
of Franklin Institute

Franklin's grave
in Christ Church
Cemetery

Photograph statues from different angles

Interior of Christ Church

234

Elfreth's Alley, the oldest
continually occupied residential
street in America, dates
back to the 1690's.

In and Around
Historic
Philadelphia

Betsy Ross House

Tomb of the Unknown Revolutionary War Soldier

The old Strasbourg
Railroad, a covered bridge
and a barn with bright
hex signs.

Longwood
Gardens

Hopewell
Village

235

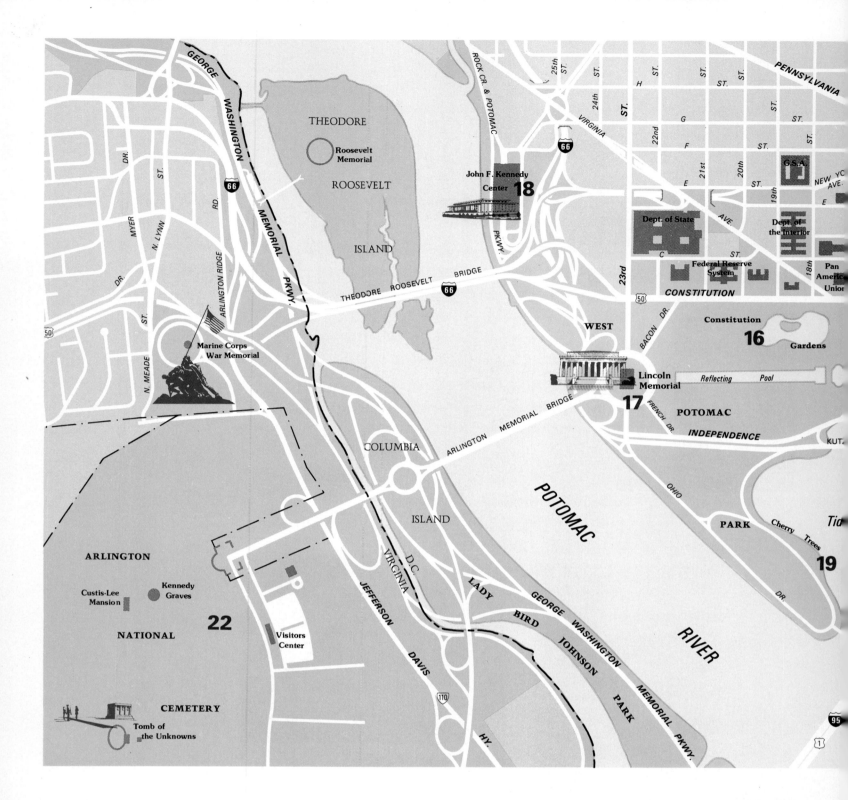

Photographing Our National Capital

Washington, D.C., is a dynamic center of history and culture. Its monuments are majestic, its pageantry colorful, and its architecture charmingly traditional. In Washington almost every moment of our past is memorialized side by side with the people and places that are making today's history.

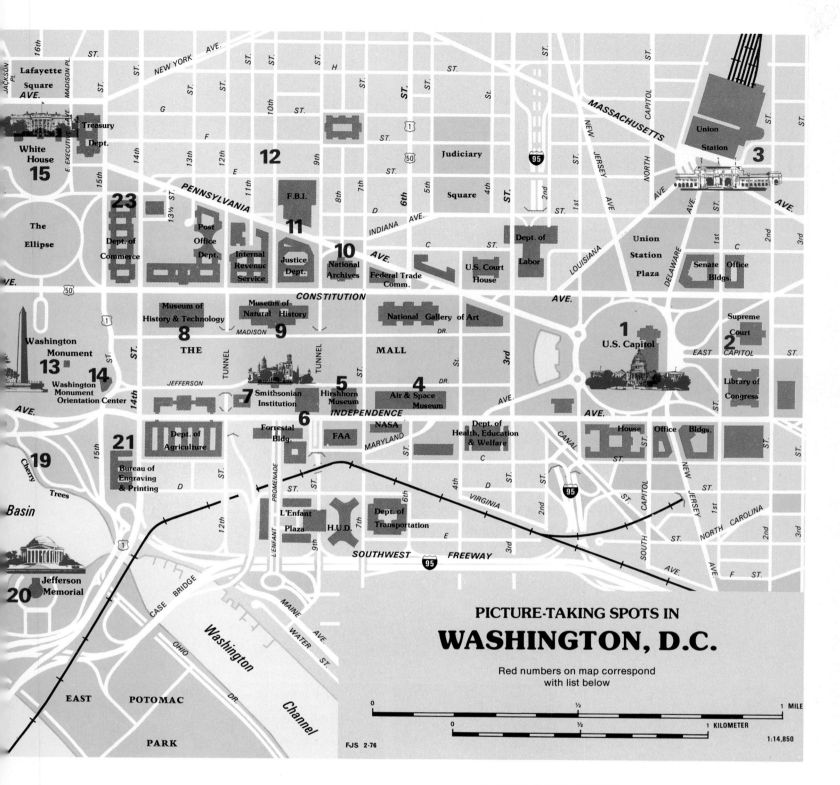

PICTURE-TAKING SPOTS IN
WASHINGTON, D.C.

Red numbers on map correspond
with list below

FJS 2-76   1:14,850

PICTURE-TAKING SPOTS

1. Capitol
2. Supreme Court
3. National Visitor's Center
4. Air and Space Museum
   and Sculpture Garden
5. Hirshhorn Museum and
   Sculpture Garden
6. Museum of Arts and Industries
7. Smithsonian Institution
8. Museum of History and
   Technology
9. Museum of Natural History
10. National Archives
11. Federal Bureau of
    Investigation

12. Ford's Theater and House
    where Lincoln died
13. Washington Monument
14. Washington Monument
    Orientation Center
15. White House
16. Constitution Gardens
17. Lincoln Memorial
18. John F. Kennedy Center
19. Cherry Blossoms (springtime)
20. Jefferson Memorial
21. Bureau of Engraving
    and Printing
22. Arlington National Cemetery
23. Bicentennial Information Center

The White House

Mount Vernon

Washington Vignettes

The Jefferson Memorial

Theodore Roosevelt Memorial

The Grave of John F. Kennedy

Tomb of the Unknown Soldier in
Arlington National Cemetery

Statue of Andrew Jackson
in Lafayette Park

United States Marine Corps War Memorial

John F. Kennedy Center for the Performing Arts

Arlington National Cemetery

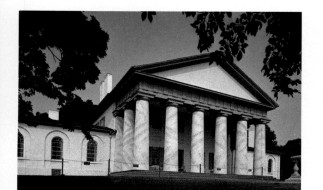

Arlington House (formerly the
Custis-Lee Mansion). Robert Lee lived
here for almost 30 years.

In Memoriam

Memorial to Mary McLeod Bethune

239

Steve Horn

We'll Rally Round the Flag

On holidays and anniversaries, for parades and pageants we see many re-enactments of historical and legendary events. In this live re-creation of the famous Iwo Jima flag-raising photo the participants were dressed in the uniforms of the Revolutionary War, the Civil War, both World Wars and the Vietnamese War.

Mount Vernon: Home of George Washington

The Washington Monument

Reflecting Pool and Lincoln Memorial

The White House

Tidal Basin and Jefferson Memorial

Mall Area and Capitol

242

Elaine Powell

The Capitol

243

The White House

Jack Zehrt

The Jefferson Memorial

247

Stinchcomb

Washington Contrasts

Some Smithsonian exhibits

The original building of
the Smithsonian Institution

The Great Falls Tavern (now a museum) is located
by the historic Chesapeake and Ohio Canal

Scene at the Hirshorn Museum
and Sculpture Garden

Springtime Cherry Blossom Festival

The great Lincoln statue designed by Daniel Chester French.

Include your family
and friends when you
take pictures of
historic monuments, statues
and buildings.

At Ford's Theatre
and Museum. The clothes that
Lincoln was wearing at the
time of his assassination.

Exterior of the Lincoln Memorial

Photographing History

Home of Frederick Douglass

Index

Steve Kelly